CONTENTS

Section

Publications

Introduction	3
Air Conditioners General Questions	6
Life Cycle Costs Questions	17
HVACR Industry Questions	21
EPA Section 608 Questions	27
Test Procedures	38
HVAC Systems Background	41
Air Conditioning and Refrigeration Calculation Questions	51
Air Conditioning System Components	54
Types of Air Conditioning Units	59
System Service and Repair Questions	64
AC Fault Diagnosis Questions	69
Refrigerant Specific Questions	72
Piping and Duct Sizing Questions	79
AC Control Systems Questions	83
HVAC Technologies Questions	86
Answers	88

Publications

Every effort has been made to ensure the information in this HVAC Exam Prep: Questions and Answers For Air Conditioning Technicians book is accurate at the time of publication. The author assumes no responsibility for omissions or errors and reserves the right to change content without notice.

The questions and answers provided in this resource are intended solely for exam preparation and training purposes and should not be considered a substitute for formal occupational HVAC training or the employer's procedures and manufacturer's instructions.

The author and publisher disclaim any liability for actions taken by individuals involved in HVAC work based on the use of this material or reliance on any references within.

It is imperative that anyone working in HVAC maintenance or installation must be formally qualified and competent. This book does not endorse or permit unqualified work in violation of legal duties.

While the guidance presented here aligns with standard HVAC practices, it is important to note that additional local or industry regulations may also apply and necessitate specific licenses or certifications. Users are strongly advised to verify all requirements applicable to their work activities and sites.

This practice question resource is designed to assist air conditioning trainees in preparing for certifications and enhancing their HVAC knowledge on the job.

However, it should not be considered a replacement for formal training programs or the acquisition of competency through experience. It is essential to stay updated with the latest HVAC best practices, standards, approvals and employers' rules to ensure continuing compliance.

Introduction

I am pleased to introduce this comprehensive book of over 300 multiple choice questions covering a wide range of topics within HVAC and specifically air conditioning and refrigeration.

Whether you are a trainee looking to expand your knowledge, a professional needing a refresher, or a manager checking your technicians' responsibilities or testing their skills, this book provides an excellent learning and revision resource.

The questions test knowledge across all key areas of HVAC including: general equipment and systems, refrigerants, combustion and ventilation, electrical controls, safety procedures, energy efficiency, maintenance best practices, plumbing, air distribution and more. The broad scope means this book is suitable for readers working in various aspects of HVAC installation, service and repair.

Each question presents a number of possible answers, with only one being correct. The options are carefully designed to be plausible to test your knowledge further. The correct answers are provided at the end of the book along with the original question for easy reference. This is very useful for self-testing and identifying areas to improve.

This question book aims to test HVAC knowledge for different types of workers including:

- Installation technicians who set up new systems
- Service technicians who maintain and repair equipment
- Ductwork specialists who work on air distribution
- Controls experts who program management systems
- Others who must follow industry standards and regulations

Many questions describe real situations you might face on the job. They don't just test facts - you need to think how codes and best practices apply to complex problems.

Tips for Using this Book Effectively:

Work through subsets of questions focusing on specific systems to target your learning. Quiz yourself regularly to reinforce knowledge.

For licensing exams or company certifications, time yourself and simulate real conditions.

Discuss the questions with coworkers to share knowledge. Great for team talks or study groups.

Managers can create tests for technicians. Monitor improvements over time.

Refer to manufacturer manuals, installation instructions or training materials to verify answers.

Consider relevant continuing education courses if you find gaps in understanding important concepts.

Using HVAC Exam Prep to Support Your Career Development

Whether just starting out or looking to advance your skills, this HVAC Exam Prep book with over 300 practice questions can aid all stages of your career training. It allows reinforcement of technical concepts covered in class. Working through subsets of HVAC Exam Prep targeted to your courses supports comprehension and exam readiness.

This HVAC Exam Prep book remains a useful study aid as a new technician. Its broad scope of multiple choice questions covering equipment, systems, controls and more helps strengthen the varied knowledge required in entry-level field roles. Referring back to areas needing improvement provides an effective way to address knowledge gaps.

For technicians gaining years of hands-on experience, this Q&A Exam Prep book questions stimulating thought on complex problems keep skills sharp. Its situations mirror those faced on job sites. Working through subsets focused on specialty areas of individual experience like combustion systems or duct design supports professional development.

All industry professionals can use HVAC Exam Prep to prepare for professional certifications demonstrating competency. Its exam-style format simulates actual testing conditions to 120 questions within 90 minutes. Identifying weak areas ahead of cert exams bolsters exam confidence and success.

Managers can assign targeted question sections from HVAC Exam Prep to technicians for skills assessments. Over time, it monitors knowledge retention and progress in maintaining expertise. Its repetitive use reinforces standards to ensure quality work.

Whether starting an HVAC career, advancing to new roles over time or working to keep skills sharp, HVAC Exam Prep's comprehensive questions at each stage of development help trainees achieve their career goals.

AIR CONDITIONERS GENERAL QUESTIONS

Question 1

Which of the following best defines "HVACR"?

A) Heating, ventilation, air-conditioning technician

B) Heating, ventilation, air-conditioning, and refrigeration

C) Heating and cooling equipment repair

D) Hydronics, ventilation, and climate regulation

Question 2

What are the three main classifications of air conditioners according to function?

A) Cooling, heating, ventilation

B) Cooling, heat pump, geothermal

C) Cooling, cooling/heating, ventilation/cooling

D) Cooling, cooling/heating, refrigeration

Question 3

What sensor controls the operation of the central air conditioning system?

A) Thermostat

B) Condensate drain

C) Liquid line

D) Filter

Question 4

Which component removes heat from the refrigerant?

A) Condenser

B) Compressor

C) Evaporator

D) Expansion valve

Question 5

What is the function of the indoor coil in the air handler unit?

A) It condenses refrigerant to release heat

B) It evaporates refrigerant to absorb heat

C) It regulates refrigerant flow

D) It controls air temperature and humidity

Question 6

What controls airflow through the evaporator coil and into the ductwork?

A) Return grille

B) Thermostat

C) Blower fan

D) Filter

Question 7

What type of air conditioner utilizes both an electric heater and a heat pump for heating?

A) Cooling only

B) Chiller

C) Cooling/heating

D) Ventilation

Question 8

What units are commonly used to measure cooling capacity?

A) Watts and RPM

B) Volts and Amps

C) Pascals and ft3/min

D) BTU/hr and Kw

Question 9

What factor most influences heating equipment size for a space?

A) Window count

B) Floor plan

C) Insulation levels

D) Duct location

Question 10

Through-the-wall units have what positioned on both the indoor and outdoor sides?

A) Coils

B) Filters

C) Fans

D) Grilles

Question 11

What type of latent heat occurs when a refrigerant changes from a gas to a liquid?

A) Condensation latent heat

B) Evaporative latent heat

C) Sensible heat

D) None of the above

Question 12

What is the standard unit of measurement in the US for heat flow?

A) Grams

B) BTU

C) Watts

D) Kcal

Question 13

What is one ton of refrigeration equivalent to in terms of cooling capacity?

A) 12,000 BTU/hr

B) 1,000 watts

C) 3,000 Kcal/hr

D) 3.517 kW

Question 14

What is relative humidity a measure of?

A) Absolute moisture content

B) Dew point temperature

C) Heat flow

D) Ratio of actual vapor pressure to saturation pressure

Question 15

How many BTUs per hour are needed to heat a typical 200 sq ft bedroom?

A) 10,000-15,000

B) 15,000-20,000

C) 20,000-25,000

D) 25,000-30,000

Question 16

What percentage of total heat loss occurs through an average home's walls?

A) 10-15%

B) 20-25%

C) 30-35%

D) 40-45%

Question 17

What determines the evaporating temperature in the evaporator coil?

A) Return air temperature

B) Superheat setting

C) Condensation temperature

D) Expansion valve setting

Question 18

What should be checked prior to any AC service call?

A) Filters

B) Ductwork

C) Wiring schematic

D) Thermostat battery

Question 19

What tool is used to recover refrigerant from an AC system?

A) Manometer

B) Vacuum pump

C) Micron gauge

D) Multi-meter

Question 20

Why is airflow volume important when servicing an AC unit?

A) Cooling capacity

B) Latent heat transfer

C) Condensate removal

D) System balance

Question 21

What should be checked when diagnosing insufficient cooling?

A) Contacts and relays

B) Fan motors and bearings

C) Superheat and subcooling

D) Ductwork integrity

Question 22

What device identifies refrigerant type in AC systems?

A) Pressure gauge

B) Manifold gauge set

C) Micron gauge

D) Recovery machine

Question 23

Which of the following would be considered personal protective equipment?

A) Manifold gauge set

B) Recovery machine

C) Safety glasses

D) Pipe cutter

Question 24

What type of equipment is required for use with ammonia refrigerant?

A) Electronic leak detector

B) Respiratory protection equipment

C) Vacuum pump

D) Tube expander

Question 25

What equipment is necessary to remove refrigerant from a system in a controlled manner?

A) Vacuum pump

B) Recovery unit

C) Manifold gauge set

D) Leak detector

Question 26

What are the three main components of a central air conditioning system?

A) Condenser, evaporator, ductwork

B) Compressor, condenser, evaporator

C) Blower, ducts, filter

D) Vents, return air grille, thermostat

Question 27

What type of protective equipment is needed when handling phoshorus or silver brazing alloys?

A) Thermal insulating gloves

B) Respirator

C) Goggles

D) Face shield

Question 28

Which tool is uniquely suited for bending soft copper refrigerant lines?

A) Tool kit for press fittings

B) Tube expander

C) Pipe bender

D) Adjustable wrench

Question 29

What type of equipment monitors for the presence of hydrocarbon refrigerants?

A) Gas detector

B) Recovery pump

C) Vacuum gauge

D) Manifold gauge set

Question 30

What attachment on a recovery machine is used to puncture access fittings to begin recovery?

A) Recovery piercing pliers

B) Suction hose

C) Charging hose

D) Vacuum hose

Question 31

What piece of auxiliary equipment is necessary to braze copper refrigerant lines?

A) Flux

B) Solder

C) Torch

D) Welder

Question 32

What type of fan is commonly used for supply air in residential ducted systems?

A) Forward curved

B) Backward inclined

C) Axial

D) Centrifugal

Question 33

What aspect of fan performance defines how much air it can move at a given power input?

A) Spindle speed

B) Blade pitch

C) Efficiency

D) Blade area

Question 34

What pump circulates hot or cold water between an air handler and connected terminals?

A) Well pump

B) Circulator pump

C) Centrifugal pump

D) Condensate pump

Question 35

What pump moves air through the indoor and outdoor coils of a split system AC?

A) Blower fan

B) Circulator pump

C) Well pump

D) Condensate pump

Question 36

What circulating pump type is continuous, quiet and self-priming for HVAC use?

A) Blower fan

B) Sump pump

C) Centrifugal pump

D) In-line pump

Question 37

What is the process of verifying and documenting that all building systems and components are installed correctly and function according to design intent?

A) Retrocommissioning

B) Tune-up

C) Commissioning

D) Calibration

Question 38

What diagnostic tools capture infrared emissions to detect thermal irregularities in HVAC equipment?

A) Data loggers

B) Ammeters

C) Combustion analyzers

D) Thermography

Question 39

What device measures amperage to identify undersized circuit breakers or overloading?

A) Dew point meter

B) Ammeter

C) Multimeter

D) Manometer

Question 40

What device measures subcooling and superheat when troubleshooting refrigerant issues?

A) Voltmeter

B) Multimeter

C) Refrigerant gauges

D) Duct blaster

Question 41

What device measures static and dynamic air pressures during ductwork testing?

A) Airflow hood

B) Psychrometer

C) Manometer

D) Anemometer

Question 42

What device passes a puff of non-toxic smoke to detect abnormal air leakage locations?

A) Infrared camera

B) Duct blaster

C) Ammeter

D) Combustion analyzer

LIFE CYCLE COSTS QUESTIONS

Question 43

Which of the following most significantly impacts the total cost of ownership over the unit's lifespan?

A) Installation costs

B) Equipment purchase price

C) Annual energy use

D) Maintenance agreements

Question 44

Replacing an evaporator coil usually occurs every _____ years on average.

A) 5-7

B) 10-12

C) 15-18

D) 20-25

Question 45

What maintenance task helps maximize equipment efficiency and lifespan?

A) Drain line cleaning

B) Capacitor replacement

C) Fan motor lubrication

D) Evaporator coil replacement

Question 46

What system upgrade usually achieves payback in 2-5 years through energy savings?

A) UV light air purifier

B) Insulated ductwork

C) Smart thermostat

D) Zoning system

Question 47

Which type of portable room air conditioner includes an optional humidification function?

A) Through-the-wall unit

B) Window unit

C) Portable evaporative cooler

D) Ductless mini-split

Question 48

What system component will typically require replacement last over the equipment's life?

A) Compressor

B) Fan motor

C) Capacitor

D) Heat exchanger

Question 49

Why is proper equipment sizing important for optimal life-cycle performance?

A) Lowers installation costs

B) Prevents short-cycling and damage

C) Improves occupant comfort

D) All of the above

Question 50

Tune-ups that include what can extend AC system life by 5-7 years?

A) Voltage checks

B) Refrigerant leak checks

C) Duct cleaning

D) Capacitor replacement

Question 51

Which type of air conditioner typically includes provisions for optional humidification?

A) Window unit

B) Ductless mini-split

C) Packaged terminal unit

D) Central air conditioning

Question 52

Improving what aspect of a home significantly improves HVAC life-cycle costs?

A) Insulation levels

B) Duct tightness

C) Window performance

D) Roof ventilation

Question 53

What maintenance tasks typically need performed quarterly?

A) Compressor tune-up and belt inspection

B) Duct sealing and zoning system check

C) Capacitor and blower motor tests

D) Filter replacement and coil cleaning

Question 54

What has the greatest influence on reducing runtime costs each month?

A) Proper sizing

B) Duct sealing

C) Equipment maintenance

D) Thermostat programming

Question 55

On average, what does replacing an old A/C unit save annually through lower utility bills?

A) $100-300

B) $300-500

C) $500-800

D) $800-1000

HVACR INDUSTRY QUESTIONS

Question 56

Which of the following best defines the role of trade associations in the HVACR industry?

A) Coordinate licensing requirements for technicians

B) Develop training and certification programs

C) Lobby for legislation on behalf of member companies

D) Set industry standards for equipment production

Question 57

Which of the following is NOT a difference between air conditioning and heating?

A) Temperature adjustment direction

B) Conditioning of air moisture

C) Fuel source

D) Primary system components

Question 58

What does "PAHRA" stand for?

A) Partnership for Air-Conditioning Hardware Regulations and Assessment

B) Partnership for Air-Conditioning and Heating Regulation Accreditation

C) Partnership for HVAC Regulations and Associated Training

D) Partnership for Airflow and Heating Regulation Authority

Question 59

Which of the following best describes the role of PAHRA in the HVACR industry?

A) Sets training requirements for HVAC programs

B) Handles licensing for HVAC technicians

C) Develops job standards for HVAC equipment manufacturers

D) Awards accreditation to education programs meeting industry standards

Question 60

Ventilation is often inadequate because:

A) Buildings have become too airtight

B) Outdoor air is too hot or cold

C) Occupant loads have increased

D) Forced air systems have replaced natural systems

Question 61

What is the primary purpose of the HVAC assessments?

A) To prepare students for industry certification exams

B) To evaluate mastery of skills for specific craft roles

C) To provide practice for competency-based education models

D) To measure a student's occupational readiness

Question 62

What is considered the high side of a refrigeration system?

A) The condenser and the liquid line

B) The compressor and the evaporator

C) The expansion valve and the suction line

D) The evaporator and the discharge line

AIR CONDITIONING SYSTEM DESIGN

Question 63

Which of the following is the most common cooling option used when conditioned air is required for an air handling unit?

A) Well water coils

B) Direct expansion coils

C) Chilled water coils

D) Air coils using site water below 65°F

Question 64

What is the main difference between air conditioning and refrigeration?

A) Air conditioning cools and dehumidifies the air, while refrigeration only cools and freezes

B) Air conditioning uses fans to circulate air, while refrigeration does not require fans

C) Air conditioning keeps the cold air close, while refrigeration pushes it away

D) Air conditioning uses coolant alone, while refrigeration also uses the air from outside

Question 65

What is a key difference between the circulation systems of air conditioning and refrigeration?

A) Air conditioning has two individual units, while refrigeration has one single unit

B) Air conditioning is designed to keep the cooled air out of the unit, while refrigeration is designed to keep the cool air within the unit

C) Air conditioning absorbs air into the system, while refrigeration is supplied with air through pipes

D) Air conditioning requires a fan, while refrigeration does not require a fan

Question 66

Which air conditioning system is suitable for providing individual temperature control in different zones or rooms, and consists of an outdoor compressor/condenser and indoor air-handling units?

A) Window Air Conditioner

B) Central Air Conditioner

C) Ductless Mini-Split

D) Portable Air Conditioner

Question 67

What should be considered when selecting the location of an outdoor unit?

A) Installing in a location with direct sunlight

B) Installing near a neighbors window

C) Installing in an area protected from wind

D) Installing at a high elevation for good air flow

Question 68

What type of refrigerant is commonly used in small air conditioning systems?

A) R-1234yf

B) R-410a

C) R-22

D) Ammonia

Question 69

What is the refrigerant known for its lower Global Warming Potential (GWP) and used as a lower GWP solution for air conditioning?

A) R-134a

B) R-32

C) R-407C

D) R-22 (Freon)

Question 70

Which of the following types of HVAC equipment is commonly used when air is cooled with 100% unconditioned outdoor air?

A) Air handling units

B) Direct evaporative cooling units

C) Water coil units

D) Refrigeration cooling units

Question 71

What is the preferred air distribution method?

A) Supply air to upper levels and return from lower levels

B) Supply air directly to generator and motor rooms

C) Circulate air lengthwise through each bay

D) Supply air to lower levels and return from upper levels

Question 72

What is the purpose of a VAV (Variable Air Volume) box in HVAC systems?

A) To control the temperature of the air

B) To regulate the airflow

C) To filter the air

D) To generate static pressure

Question 73

Which of the following locations is recommended by the document for intake louvers?

A) Near light fixtures

B) Opposite heat sources

C) Near air exhaust openings

D) Below roof level

Question 74

Complete HVAC system redundancy generally involves:

A) Two equally sized systems capable of the full load

B) Dedicated HVAC equipment for each room

C) Automatic switching controls for backup equipment

D) Systems sized at 50-75% of total capacity

Question 75

What scale is used to rate the moisture removal capacity of air conditioners and dehumidifiers?

A) SEER rating

B) Pints per day

C) BTU/hr

D) EER

Question 76

What component found in some PTAC units improves dehumidification performance?

A) Disposable filter

B) Reed switch

C) Dehumidifying coil

D) Bypass damper

EPA SECTION 608 QUESTIONS

Question 77

Which of the following best describes the type of refrigerant that has been shown to be the most destructive to stratospheric ozone?

A) Refrigerants that contain fluorine and hydrogen.

B) Refrigerants containing only chlorine.

C) Refrigerants that are stable and do not break down in the lower atmosphere.

D) Refrigerants containing bromine.

Question 78

EPA regulations require technicians to demonstrate the ability to perform which refrigerant handling procedure?

A) Recovery

B) Reclaiming

C) Leak detection

D) Proper oil changing

Question 79

What is the term used to describe the purity standard refrigerant must meet to be considered reclaimed?

A) ARI-700 standard

B) R-410A standard

C) HFC-134a standard

D) CFC-12 standard

Question 80

According to the Montreal Protocol, which of the following substances is NOT controlled?

A) Hydrochlorofluorocarbons

B) Chlorofluorocarbons

C) Carbon dioxide

D) Halons

Question 81

What is the length of time refrigerant recovered from a system less than 1 year old can be called reclaimed?

A) 1 month

B) 6 months

C) It can never be called reclaimed

D) 1 year

Question 82

Which part of a vapor compression system changes the low pressure vapor to a high pressure vapor?

A) Condenser

B) Expansion device

C) Receiver

D) Compressor

Question 83

Which of the following best describes an azeotropic refrigerant mixture?

A) A mixture that always contains at least three components

B) A mixture with different boiling points at various pressures

C) A mixture that acts as a single component refrigerant

D) A mixture that is always 50% of each component

Question 84

Which of the following is true about blended refrigerants leaking from a system?

A) They leak at an even rate

B) They leak slower than other refrigerants

C) They leak faster than other refrigerants

D) They only leak if a joint completely fails

Question 85

Which of the following devices is used to reduce the pressure of refrigerant vapor?

A) Compressor

B) Expansion device

C) Receiver

D) Evaporator

Question 86

What does an HFC refrigerant contain?

A) Hydrogen, fluorine, carbon

B) Chlorine, fluorine, calcium

C) Oxygen, nitrogen, carbon

D) Helium, fluorine, hydrogen

Question 87

According to the EPA, when must an oil sample be taken from a system?

A) When a new filter drier is installed

B) During every routine maintenance

C) When the system is underperforming

D) After a major leak or component failure

Question 88

What type of refrigerant requires the most amount of pressure to change from a liquid to a vapor?

A) HCFC

B) HFC

C) CFC

D) Natural refrigerants

Question 89

Which part of a vapor compression system converts high pressure vapor back to high pressure liquid?

A) Compressor

B) Condenser

C) Evaporator

D) Expansion device

Question 90

Which of the following best describes the motive behind the Montreal Protocol?

A) To control greenhouse gas emissions

B) To set international energy efficiency standards

C) To control the production of ozone depleting substances

D) To ban the use of vapor compression technology

Question 91

Which of the following parts would not be considered required by EPA regulations for all air conditioning and refrigeration systems using CFCs, HCFCs or HFCs?

A) Thermostatic expansion valve

B) Compressor

C) Filter drier

D) Service valve port

Question 92

What is the term used to describe the process of cleaning a refrigerant to reduce moisture and acidity?

A) Recovery

B) Reclamation

C) Recycling

D) Reprocessing

Question 93

What type of equipment relies on the compressor in the existing system to perform recovery?

A) Self-contained recovery units

B) System-dependent recovery units

C) Recovery containers

D) System-independent recovery machines

Question 94

According to ASHRAE safety classification, which designation indicates the most unsafe refrigerant?

A) A-1

B) B-1

C) A-3

D) B-3

Question 95

When would it be acceptable to vent small amounts of refrigerant according to EPA regulations?

A) When adding nitrogen for leak testing

B) When pumping down the system before repair

C) In the normal operation of an appliance

D) When recovering refrigerant from small appliances

Question 96

Which of the following best describes the requirement for hydrostatic testing of reusable cylinders?

A) Every 2 years

B) Every 5 years

C) Only if pressurized above 15 psig

D) Annually

Question 97

Which part of a vapor compression system absorbs heat from the refrigerated space?

A) Compressor

B) Evaporator

C) Condenser

D) Receiver

Question 98

What is the term used to describe the process that returns refrigerant to new product specifications through chemical analysis and purity testing?

A) Recovery

B) Reclamation

C) Recycling

D) Recharging

Question 99

What is considered the most effective method for detecting small refrigerant leaks according to the EPA?

A) Halide torch

B) Smell test

C) Electronic or ultrasonic detection

D) Bubble solution application

Question 100

How many ozone molecules can each chlorine atom in the stratosphere destroy?

A) 10

B) 100

C) 1,000

D) 100,000

Question 101

Which of the following best characterizes a self-contained recovery device?

A) Requires the compressor in the system to function

B) Can capture refrigerant in liquid or vapor form without external equipment

C) Has a power source that requires charging

D) Can only be used on small equipment under 15 pounds

Question 102

What is the term used to describe the quantitative rating of a refrigerant's ability to deplete stratospheric ozone?

A) Global warming potential

B) Ozone depletion potential

C) Atmospheric lifetime

D) Air conditioning efficiency

Question 103

What should Technicians never do when using dry nitrogen to pressurize a system?

A) Charge as a liquid

B) Apply below 50 PSIG pressure

C) Use an oxygen regulator

D) Apply without a pressure regulator

Question 104

What device is used to safely reduce the pressure in a refrigerant cylinder before disposal?

A) Recovery machine

B) Manifold gauge set

C) Pressure regulator

D) Vacuum pump

Question 105

Which of the following best characterizes a non-azeotropic refrigerant mixture?

A) Acts as a single component

B) Consists of two components

C) Has a single boiling point

D) Composition changes with temperature

Question 106

What should technicians do before opening a refrigeration system or disposing of its components?

A) Recover any remaining refrigerant

B) Dehydrate the system

C) Conduct an airflow test

D) Add compressor oil

Question 107

Which of the following is used to improve the sensitivity of leak detectors?

A) Bromomethane tracer gas

B) Helium

C) Nitrogen

D) Carbon monoxide

Question 108

When should an oil sample be taken from a system according to EPA guidelines?

A) Monthly

B) After a catastrophic failure

C) After 500 hours of operation

D) During routine maintenance

Question 109

What is considered the proper method of removing all refrigerant from a system or component?

A) Bubble evacuation

B) Pressurized nitrogen purge

C) Evacuation to a hard vacuum

D) Reverse flow recovery

Question 110

What type of equipment can capture refrigerant in either liquid or vapor form without relying on system components?

A) System-dependent recovery units

B) Recovery cylinders

C) System-independent recovery machines

D) Reusable recovery tanks

Question 111

Non-condensable gases such as air prevent which part of the vapor compression process from working properly?

A) Compression

B) Condensation

C) Evaporation

D) Expansion

Question 112

According to the Montreal Protocol, which is considered less damaging to stratospheric ozone than CFCs?

A) HFCs

B) HFCS

C) HCFCs

D) Natural refrigerants

Question 113

What type of halogenated substance is R-141b?

A) HCFC

B) CFC

C) HFC

D) Halon

Question 114

When using compressed gas for leak detection or system pressure, technicians should use:

A) Carbon dioxide

B) Oxygen

C) Helium

D) Nitrogen

Question 115

Which component commonly causes moisture to migrate into the compressor crankcase?

A) Condenser

B) Filter drier

C) Thermostatic expansion valve

D) Evaporator

Question 116

What term describes the process of achieving a vacuum that prohibits the flow of air and non-condensable gases into the system?

A) Dehydration

B) Purging

C) Evacuation

D) Recovery

Question 117

When should recovery and recycling equipment be certified according to the EPA?

A) Every 3 years

B) Only at initial purchase

C) Annually

D) Every 5 years

TEST PROCEDURES

Question 118

According to the current test procedures, which of the following split system types can be tested?

A) Only single-split systems

B) Multi-split, multi-head mini-split, and multi-circuit systems

C) Only multi-circuit systems

D) No split systems are covered

Question 119

Testing variable capacity AC units at part load conditions according to the US test procedure has proven:

A) Simple and accurate

B) Accurate but requires manufacturer control inputs

C) Problematic and inaccurate

D) Not addressed by the current procedure

Question 120

What does 10 CFR 430 Subpart B primarily address?

A) Energy consumption of household appliances

B) Safety regulations for industrial machinery

C) Construction standards for residential buildings

D) Environmental impact of transportation systems

Question 121

What is the document that provides detailed inspection checklists and test worksheets for the functional inspection and testing of HVAC systems?

A) Acceptance Testing Procedures for Heating, Ventilating, and Air-Conditioning Systems

B) HVAC Functional Inspection and Testing Guide

C) Testing & Commissioning Procedure for Air-conditioning, Refrigeration, Ventilation, and Central Monitoring & Control System Installation

D) Uniform Mechanical Code

Question 122

Which of the following refrigerants has the highest critical pressure?

A) R-12

B) Ammonia

C) R-11

D) R-22

Question 123

Where does the lowest temperature occur in a vapour compression cycle?

A) Compressor

B) Condenser

C) Evaporator

D) Expansion valve

Question 124

What is the leading efficiency metric used for minimum standards and energy guide labels for room air conditioners?

A) Seasonal Coefficient of Performance (SCOP)

B) Energy Efficiency Ratio (EER)

C) Seasonal Energy Efficiency Ratio (SEER)

D) Coefficient of Performance (COP)

Question 125

What governs heat transfer through convection?

A) Density differences

B) Electromagnetic waves

C) Molecular vibration

D) Thermal conductivity

Question 126

What is the purpose of the cycling test in air conditioner testing?

A) To measure the air conditioner's weight

B) To assess the system's performance during part-load operation and temperature changes

C) To determine the color of the air conditioner

D) To evaluate the air conditioner's sound levels

HVAC SYSTEMS BACKGROUND

Question 127

What is the unit of heat?

A) Watt

B) Joule

C) BTU

D) Pascal

Question 128

Which of the following is NOT a mechanism of heat transfer?

A) Conduction

B) Convection

C) Evaporation

D) Illumination

Question 129

Which of the following best defines the humidity ratio?

A) Weight of water vapor per unit weight of dry air

B) Moisture content by mass of moist air

C) Density of water vapor per volume of dry air

D) Vapor pressure of saturated air at a given temperature

Question 130

What temperature scale has its freezing point defined at 0°C and boiling point at 100°C?

A) Fahrenheit

B) Rankine

C) Kelvin

D) Celsius

Question 131

What is the room sensible heat factor used for in air conditioning systems?

A) Measuring the heat produced by electronic devices

B) Calculating the heat gain from occupants and lights

C) Assessing the heat exchange in the room

D) Determining the efficiency of the HVAC system

Question 132

What is the primary factor that influences the design of an AC system in a residential setting?

A) Energy efficiency

B) Cost-effectiveness

C) Type and size of the system

D) Cooling loads

Question 133

Which of the following is essential for ensuring good indoor air quality and efficient air distribution in an AC system design?

A) Health and safety requirements

B) Ventilation and ducts

C) Energy efficiency

D) Cost-effectiveness

Question 134

What is the purpose of equipment sizing in the design of an AC system?

A) To ensure proper ventilation

B) To balance initial cost with long-term savings

C) To determine the type and size of the system

D) To comply with health and safety standards

Question 135

What type of heat is involved when a refrigerant changes from a gas to a liquid?

A) Latent heat

B) Conduction heat

C) Radiant heat

D) Sensible heat

Question 136

Why is proper ductwork design important in the AC system design for a residential setting?

A) To reduce electricity consumption

B) To ensure compliance with health and safety standards

C) To achieve even comfort throughout the home

D) To balance the initial cost of the system with long-term savings

Question 137

Which type of AC system has two units for cooling and heating, and is commonly found in residential settings?

A) Traditional Split System

B) Central Air Conditioning

C) Packaged Air Conditioning

D) Ductless Mini-Split System

Question 138

Which type of air conditioning system is often used in residential settings where space for indoor components is limited?

A) Central Air Conditioner

B) Ductless Mini-Split

C) Window Air Conditioner

D) Packaged System

Question 139

Which of the following best defines sensible heat?

A) Heat that increases temperature but not humidity

B) Heat that changes phase from solid to liquid

C) Heat related to moisture content of air

D) Heat required to maintain indoor comfort levels

Question 140

Sensible heat is determined by which property of air?

A) Temperature

B) Humidity ratio

C) Enthalpy

D) Density

Question 141

What is the temperature range of the standard psychrometric chart for air conditioning?

A) 0 to 50°C

B) 32 to 80°F

C) -20 to 40°C

D) 32 to 120°F

Question 142

Which of the following is NOT one of the purposes of an HVAC system?

A) Provide temperature control

B) Ensure proper ventilation

C) Increase relative humidity

D) Provide moisture control

Question 143

Which psychrometric process increases both temperature and moisture content?

A) Cooling

B) Heating

C) Dehumidification

D) Humidification

Question 144

What is considered the boundary that separates the indoor and outdoor environment?

A) Building air barrier

B) Insulation layer

C) Thermal boundary

D) Pressure boundary

Question 145

What type of ventilation strategy utilizes both supply and exhaust fans?

A) Exhaust-only

B) Balanced

C) Supply-only

D) Indoor air quality

Question 146

Which of the following best summarizes the primary function of an HVAC system?

A) To supply different environmental conditions for various industrial processes.

B) To maintain occupant comfort in a conditioned space.

C) To heat and cool large buildings efficiently.

D) To remove heat and humidity from indoor spaces.

Question 147

Which of the following is NOT a consideration in properly designing an air conditioning system?

A) Building orientation

B) Expected occupancy schedule

C) Cost of annual maintenance

D) Type of wall construction

Question 148

What year did the American Society of Heating and Ventilating Engineers (ASH&VE) form?

A) 1894

B) 1904

C) 1908

D) 1959

Question 149

What was one of the earliest key developments in improving combustion heating systems according to the passage?

A) Addition of fans to furnace systems

B) Use of condensate pumps in steam systems

C) Conversion to oil and gas firing

D) Insulation of radiator enclosures

Question 150

Which of the following best defines the Energy Star program mentioned in the passage?

A) A voluntary certification for green buildings

B) A requirement for buildings to meet ASHRAE energy standards

C) An energy budget approach to building design

D) A standard that rates building energy performance compared to national averages

Question 151

Which of the following factors would NOT affect the performance of an HVAC system?

A) Number of occupants

B) Lighting load

C) Insulation levels

D) Amount of outdoor shade trees

Question 152

Which type of ventilation system removes air from specific rooms or areas using a local exhaust fan?

A) Supply ventilation

B) Balanced ventilation

C) Spot ventilation

D) Whole house ventilation

Question 153

Which type of HVAC system provides conditioned air to each room using supply and return registers?

A) Forced air system

B) Heat pump

C) Geothermal system

D) Radiant system

Question 154

Which of the following is NOT considered an important design concept for energy efficient design?

A) Understanding the relationship between energy and power

B) Maintaining complexity

C) Using self-imposed budgets

D) Applying energy-smart design practices

Question 155

Which of the following is considered a key element of sustainable design?

A) Daylighting

B) Efficient use of materials

C) Reduced water use

D) Efficient use of energy resources

Question 156

Which of the following best defines the LEED program?

A) A standard for green product certification

B) A voluntary standard for sustainable building design and construction

C) A requirement to meet ASHRAE energy codes

D) Defines what makes a building energy efficient

Question 157

According to the second law of thermodynamics, which of the following cannot occur naturally without effort expended somewhere?

A) Heat transfer from a hot body to a cold body

B) The mixing of two gases

C) A chemical reaction

D) Heat transfer from a colder body to a hotter body

Question 158

Which process/scenario BEST represents an irreversible process?

A) The natural mixing of two gases in contact

B) The reversible transfer of heat between two bodies at the same temperature

C) A thermodynamic cycle that returns a system to its initial state

D) An idealized, quasi-static process that can be reversed by an infinitesimal change in conditions

Question 159

Which of the following processes involves NO transfer of heat?

A) Isobaric

B) Isothermal

C) Adiabatic

D) Isentropic

Question 160

Below which pressure does water NOT exist in three phases (solid, liquid, vapor) at the same temperature?

A) Sublimation pressure

B) Triple point pressure

C) Critical pressure

D) Fusion pressure

Question 161

What is meant by the term "intensive property" as used in thermodynamics?

A) A property that depends on the amount of matter in the system

B) A property whose value is independent of the size or extent of the system

C) A property whose value depends on the path taken between initial and final states

D) A property that is defined in terms of other properties

Question 162

Which of the following scales uses degrees K as its absolute temperature units?

A) Kelvin

B) Celsius

C) Fahrenheit

D) Rankine

Question 163

What type of HVAC system design method determines room-by-room heating and cooling loads?

A) Manual D

B) Manual J

C) Manual S

D) Standard 152

AIR CONDITIONING AND REFRIGERATION CALCULATION QUESTIONS

Question 164

What is the base unit used for measuring heat in the HVAC industry?

A) Watts

B) Joules

C) Calories

D) BTUs

Question 165

What is the specific heat of air in Btu/lb°F?

A) 0.24

B) 1.08

C) 1.3

D) 4.5

Question 166

What constant pressure is used to define 1 Ton of Refrigeration?

A) 30 inHg

B) 14.7 psi

C) 1 atm

D) 29.92 inHg

Question 167

What constant is used to determine the latent heat load in Btu/h using the formula:

Latent Load = Constant x CFM x (Wo - Wi)?

A) 4.5

B) 1.08

C) 0.68

D) 1,060

Question 168

What is the typical CFM produced per ton of air conditioning?

A) 300 CFM

B) 450 CFM

C) 550 CFM

D) 400 CFM

Question 169

What value is used for air density in most HVAC calculations in lb/ft3?

A) 0.9

B) 0.075

C) 0.06

D) 0.15

Question 170

What variable is defined as the ratio of vapor pressure to the saturation vapor pressure?

A) Absolute humidity

B) Specific humidity

C) Relative humidity

D) Density

Question 171

What is considered the minimum CFM of airflow per 100 square feet of house floor area for proper HVAC performance?

A) 25-50 CFM

B) 50-75 CFM

C) 75-100 CFM

D) 100-150 CFM

Question 172

Which of the following is NOT considered a good location for an indoor air conditioning unit?

A) Near a window for good air circulation

B) In an area with a lot of dust and smoke

C) In a kitchen near cooking appliances

D) In a bathroom prone to high moisture

Question 173

Which of the following is NOT an appropriate outdoor air design temperature to use for HVAC cooling load calculations?

A) 2-1/2 percent value

B) 99 percent value

C) Extreme design conditions

D) Median value

Question 174

What calculation determines BTUs contained in 1 pound of a substance with a given specific heat?

A) BTU = Mass x Specific Heat x Temperature Change

B) BTU = Temperature x Temperature Change

C) BTU = Heat of Vaporization x Pounds

D) BTU = Enthalpy x Specific Volume

Question 175

Heat flows naturally from objects at what temperature to objects at what lower temperature?

A) Cooler to warmer

B) Lighter to heavier

C) Higher to lower

D) Decreases to increases

AIR CONDITIONING SYSTEM COMPONENTS

Question 176

What device senses and controls room temperature?

A) Thermostat

B) Contactor

C) Timer

D) Transformer

Question 177

What type of compressor is commonly used in air conditioners?

A) Centrifugal compressor

B) Axial flow compressor

C) Reciprocating compressor

D) Scroll compressor

Question 178

What component is located entirely on the interior side of the wall?

A) Compressor

B) Condenser coil

C) Fan motor

D) Evaporator coil

Question 179

What device regulates the flow of refrigerant into the evaporator?

A) Capillary tube

B) Condenser

C) Check valve

D) Accumulator

Question 180

What is the purpose of a strainer in an AC system?

A) To remove moisture from the refrigerant

B) To regulate refrigerant flow

C) To remove foreign particles from the refrigerant

D) To absorb vibration

Question 181

What allows the compressor to start under high load conditions?

A) Transformer

B) Timer

C) Hard start kit

D) Reversing valve

Question 182

What device protects the compressor from overload?

A) Capacitor

B) Thermostat

C) Overload protector

D) Accumulator

Question 183

What device senses room temperature and controls the compressor?

A) Thermistor

B) Capillary tube

C) Check valve

D) Overload protector

Question 184

What determines the evaporating temperature of the refrigerant in the evaporator?

A) Condensing pressure

B) Suction pressure

C) Discharge pressure

D) Saturated temperature

Question 185

How are indoor units typically installed?

A) Ducted into the ceiling

B) Mounted on an exterior wall

C) Suspended from the ceiling

D) Installed in a window

Question 186

What tool is used to accurately measure refrigerant pressures?

A) Continuity tester

B) Hook gauge

C) Clamp meter

D) Manometer

Question 187

When installing an indoor unit, what is important to consider for adequate air circulation?

A) Installing near a window

B) Minimum specified clearance

C) Mounting height

D) Drain line placement

Question 188

What type of thermostat directly controls single speed compressor units?

A) Electronic

B) Pneumatic

C) Solid state

D) Mechanical

Question 189

What device is used to control the flow of liquid refrigerant into the evaporator?

A) Condenser

B) Compressor

C) Thermostat

D) Expansion Valve

Question 190

What process causes the high pressure refrigerant liquid to change to low pressure in the capillary tube?

A) Evaporation

B) Condensation

C) Compression

D) Expansion

Question 191

What type of heat is released in the condenser?

A) Latent heat

B) Radiant heat

C) Conduction heat

D) Sensible heat

Question 192

What device is used to separate any liquid refrigerant from the suction line vapor before entering the compressor?

A) Accumulator

B) Condenser

C) Receiver

D) Strainer

Question 193

What property of R-22 allows it to absorb a large amount of heat with little rise in temperature in the evaporator?

A) High density

B) Low boiling point

C) High heat of vaporization

D) High thermal conductivity

Question 194

What component receives the high pressure, high temperature vapor from the condenser?

A) Expansion valve

B) Receiver

C) Compressor

D) Evaporator

Question 195

What causes an increase in pressure when the refrigerant is compressed in the compressor?

A) Latent heat

B) Volume decrease

C) Temperature increase

D) Phase change

TYPES OF AIR CONDITIONING UNITS

Question 196

What allows installation and removal of a window unit from the outside of a building?

A) Sliding frame assembly

B) Adjustable louvers

C) Fresh air vent

D) Foam insulation

Question 197

What device controls moisture removal in the indoor coil of a window unit?

A) Condenser fan

B) Evaporator coil

C) Check valve

D) Dehumidistat

Question 198

What device controls the degree of air circulation throughout a room?

A) Thermostat

B) Dehumidistat

C) Condenser fan

D) Louver blades

Question 199

Where is the thermostat sensor typically located on a window unit?

A) Behind air filter

B) Inside the indoor coil

C) Near the evaporator coil

D) On the refrigerant lines

Question 200

What is the recommended first step before purchasing a window air conditioning unit for your home?

A) Measure the size and shape of your windows

B) Determine the smart features available

C) Assess the position and voltage of nearby electrical outlets

D) Calculate the target coverage area in square feet

Question 201

What is the common cause of leaking water in a window air conditioning unit?

A) Dirty filter

B) Excessive cycling

C) Air leaks

D) Condensation on the evaporator coil

Question 202

What is the recommended action to prevent air leaks when installing a window air conditioning unit?

A) Use a voltage stabilizer

B) Seal the window with accordion panels

C) Vent the exhaust hose through a hole in the wall

D) Direct the exhaust hose away from the open window

Question 203

Which of the following is a unique element of split air conditioners?

A) They have to be drained periodically

B) They can be used for the same purposes as window AC units

C) They are the noisiest type of air conditioners

D) They do not require regular maintenance

Question 204

What is one of the main advantages of a multi split system air conditioner?

A) It is the noisiest part of the air conditioner

B) It can only cool the rooms you need to, saving money and energy

C) It requires a separate outdoor unit for each indoor unit

D) It has built-in timers and different controls to personalize the experience

Question 205

What is a common problem that can arise due to irregular maintenance of a split air conditioner?

A) Overcooling of the room

B) High refrigerant levels

C) Lack of cooling

D) Faulty compressor

Question 206

What is a characteristic of the outdoor unit in a split air conditioning system?

A) It only contains the fan

B) It houses the compressor and condenser

C) It is responsible for indoor air circulation

D) It controls the temperature settings

Question 207

What type of fan is commonly used in indoor split units?

A) Cross flow

B) Centrifugal

C) Axial

D) Tangential

Question 208

What provides auxiliary heating for certain split systems?

A) Heat pump

B) Electric coil

C) Gas furnace

D) Geothermal exchange

Question 209

What type of resistance heating element is common for auxiliary heat?

A) Radiant

B) Infrared

C) Quartz

D) Calrod

Question 210

What type of HVAC system contains all refrigerant circuit components within one factory-made enclosure?

A) Split system

B) Window unit

C) Packaged terminal AC

D) Ductless mini split

Question 211

What type of piping is typically used for refrigerant lines in packaged units?

A) Flexible hoses

B) Brazed joints

C) Flared fittings

D) Screwed connections

Question 212

How is conditioned air distributed from packaged terminal ACs?

A) Wall sleeves

B) Ceiling grille

C) Direct blow

D) Ductwork

Question 213

What allows packaged rooftop units to cool multiple zones?

A) Variable speed fan

B) Auxiliary heat option

C) Fresh air intake

D) Water-cooled condenser

Question 214

What directs air into the building through a ceiling tile or wall sleeve?

A) Return grille

B) Supply plenum

C) Fresh air damper

D) Discharge grille

Question 215

What devices sense return air conditions on some packaged units?

A) Thermistors

B) Solenoid valves

C) Relays

D) Controllers

SYSTEM SERVICE AND REPAIR QUESTIONS

Question 216

Why should non-condensibles be removed prior to system repair?

A) Prevent compressor damage

B) Improper oil return

C) Inhibit heat transfer

D) Cause valve freeze-up

Question 217

What is used to convert a system to an alternative refrigerant?

A) Replacement

B) Retrofit kit

C) Recovery cylinder

D) Service valve

Question 218

Why should lubricant be changed during retrofit procedures?

A) Incompatibility with new refrigerant

B) Requirements for POE oil

C) Ensure proper viscosity

D) Prevent cross-contamination

Question 219

What information is required for environmentally responsible reclamation?

A) Recovery method

B) Retrofit procedure

C) Refrigerant composition

D) End-of-life equipment

Question 220

What causes the pressure on the high side of an air conditioning system to rise rapidly leading to a condition known as "slugging"?

A) Clogged filter/drier

B) Undercharged refrigerant

C) Open thermostatic expansion valve

D) Non-condensable gases

Question 221

What component acts as a sort of "shock absorber" in an air conditioning system and allows the compressor to operate smoothly by temporarily storing excess refrigerant during off cycles?

A) Thermal expansion valve

B) Suction accumulator

C) Compressor

D) Receiver

Question 222

What is the purpose of the sight glass installed on the liquid line just before the thermostatic expansion valve in an air conditioning system?

A) Indicates refrigerant charge level

B) Allows oil to pass through

C) Catches particulates

D) Controls refrigerant flow

Question 223

What is the normal operating pressure range at ambient temperature of 90°F for an R-22 air conditioning system with a 15 SEER rating?

A) 175-225 psig

B) 125-150 psig

C) 225-275 psig

D) 75-100 psig

Question 224

What causes abnormally high head (high side) pressure in an air conditioning system?

A) Undercharged refrigerant

B) Clogged filter/drier

C) Non-condensable gases

D) Low ambient temperature

Question 225

What component detects excessively low or high refrigerant pressures and shuts down the compressor for safety?

A) Pressure transducer

B) Pressure control switch

C) Thermostat

D) Compressor internal overload

Question 226

What condition or defect would cause the evaporator coil leaving air temperature to be warmer than normal?

A) Overcharged system

B) Dirty condenser coils

C) Low refrigerant charge

D) Undersized condenser

Question 227

What are small ports or holes connected to suction and discharge lines of an air conditioning compressor used for?

A) Cooling oil circulation

B) Pressure regulation

C) Oil equalization

D) Refrigerant metering

Question 228

An accumulation of what substance on outdoor AC units reduces efficiency by preventing heat transfer?

A) Algae

B) Rust

C) Dirt

D) Mineral deposits

Question 229

During a/c system repair, what should be performed prior to evacuating moisture from the system?

A) Replacing drier

B) Adding refrigerant

C) Cleaning coils

D) Recovering refrigerant

Question 230

What type of filter is typically found in an indoor air handler or furnace to catch dust and debris from returning air?

A) Electrostatic

B) HEPA

C) Pleated paper

D) Washable mesh

Question 231

What device protects the compressor from liquid refrigerant by temporarily storing it during off cycles?

A) Accumulator

B) Oil equalizer

C) Condenser coil

D) Filter/drier

Question 232

What is the most common cause of air conditioning compressor failure?

A) Electrical issues

B) Lack of maintenance

C) Overcharging

D) Refrigerant leaks

Question 233

What device uses subcooling to regulate refrigerant flow into an evaporator coil?

A) TXV

B) Piston valve

C) Solenoid valve

D) Thermistor

AC FAULT DIAGNOSIS QUESTIONS

Question 234

What is the most likely cause if an AC unit trips the breaker whenever turned on?

A) Damaged start capacitor

B) Low refrigerant charge

C) Dirty condenser coils

D) Clogged filters

Question 235

A home AC unit is producing warm air from vents. What should be checked first?

A) Ductwork insulation

B) Fan blade alignment

C) Thermostat calibration

D) Capacitor ratings

Question 236

AC runs but the home does not cool down. What is a possible cause?

A) Loose electrical connections

B) Refrigerant leak

C) Low air filter restriction

D) Tripped pressure switch

Question 237

AC unit blows warm air on one side of home. What diagnostic step should be taken?

A) Inspect return ducts

B) Check refrigerant level

C) Test wiring connections

D) Examine zone dampers

Question 238

AC unit blows humid air and water droplets form on supply vents. What is likely faulty?

A) Condenser fan motor

B) Drain line restriction

C) Compressor valves

D) Low side pressure

Question 239

AC unit frequently cycles on and off. What can potentially remedy this?

A) Clean condenser coils

B) Replace thermostat

C) Check superheat setting

D) Tighten electrical connections

Question 240

AC unit blows warm air and makes buzzing noise. What component may be faulty?

A) Blower motor

B) Evaporator coils

C) Contactor points

D) Capacitor

Question 241

AC unit blows warm air with ice forming on evap coils. What should be checked?

A) Airflow across coils

B) TXV operation

C) Subcooling levels

D) Cold suction line

Question 242

AC unit blows 70 degrees air on warm days. What may cause this?

A) Dirty air filter

B) Low side undercharge

C) Thermostat stuck closed

D) Contactor defect

Question 243

AC unit blows warm air when changing to cool mode. First inspect which component?

A) Filter

B) Condenser fan

C) Fan coil unit

D) Temperature sensors

Question 244

On a hot day, the system pressure rises high but cycling cutout doesn't function. What could be faulty?

A) Fan blade

B) Thermostat

C) Contactor

D) High pressure control

Question 245

The AC unit blows 66°F air on 95°F day. Subcooling is normal but suction pressure is low. What could be the problem?

A) Leaking TXV

B) Clogged condenser

C) Low superheat

D) Undercharged refrigerant

REFRIGERANT SPECIFIC QUESTIONS

Question 246

Which ISO standard addresses the designation and classification of refrigerants?

A) ISO 817

B) ISO 5149

C) ISO 916

D) EN 13313

Question 247

What does ISO 916 cover in relation to refrigeration systems?

A) Basic requirements

B) Design and construction

C) Safety performance testing

D) Technical performance testing

Question 248

What does the LFL value indicate for refrigerant flammability classification?

A) Heat of combustion

B) Lowest concentration required for ignition

C) Flammability range

D) Maximum recommended concentration

Question 249

Is it possible for a refrigerant to be considered non-toxic?

A) Yes

B) No

C) Only slightly toxic

D) Below a certain TLV-TWA level

Question 250

What standard does the refrigerant numbering classification system follow?

A) ISO 817

B) EN 378

C) ASHRAE 34

D) IIR Standard

Question 251

Which lubricant property aims to prevent plugging of refrigerant control components?

A) Low wax content

B) Low pour point

C) Low viscosity index

D) Good miscibility

Question 252

Which property maintains good lubrication at high and low temperatures?

A) Good miscibility

B) Low pour point

C) Low viscosity index

D) Good thermal stability

Question 253

What is the overall goal of containment and leak detection?

A) Locate system problems

B) Improve system efficiency

C) Minimize refrigerant releases

D) Identify required repairs

Question 254

According to the ISO 11650 standard, what does recovery involve?

A) Removing refrigerant and storing it externally

B) Extracting and cleaning refrigerant at a job site

C) Processing refrigerant for reuse in equipment

D) Purifying contaminated refrigerant

Question 255

How is recovered refrigerant stored according to the same standard as above?

A) In drums

B) In cylinders

C) In situ

D) Externally to the system

Question 256

Where does recycling typically take place?

A) In a laboratory

B) At a refrigerant reclamation facility

C) At the field job site

D) During system manufacture

Question 257

What is the primary purpose of refrigerant recovery equipment?

A) To permanently destroy refrigerants

B) To recycle refrigerants for reuse

C) To temporarily store recovered refrigerant

D) To remove moisture from refrigerants

Question 258

Which method of refrigerant recovery is recommended for liquid refrigerant transfer from an AC system?

A) Vapour transfer

B) Manifold gauging

C) Push-pull transfer

D) Pumpdown recovery

Question 259

What is the purpose of purging in the servicing of a refrigeration system?

A) To remove non-condensable gases

B) To increase the system pressure

C) To prevent oil contamination

D) To reduce the refrigerant flow

Question 260

When charging refrigerants, why is it important to follow the manufacturer's specifications?

A) To save time and effort

B) To increase the system pressure

C) To ensure proper system performance and efficiency

D) To avoid using the correct tools

Question 261

Which of the following is a purpose of flaring in tubing techniques for refrigeration systems?

A) To reduce the tubing size

B) To prevent oil contamination

C) To create a seal with another fitting

D) To increase the refrigerant flow

Question 262

What is the main function of a manifold gauge in refrigeration servicing?

A) To measure the refrigerant charge by weight

B) To monitor the system's temperature

C) To control the refrigerant flow

D) To measure the system's pressure

Question 263

What is the main reason why moisture is difficult to eliminate from a refrigeration system?

A) It is essentially dissolved in the refrigerant

B) It evaporates at a very low temperature

C) It reacts with the refrigerant to form a protective layer

D) It is constantly replenished by the lubricant

Question 264

What can happen if the moisture concentration in a refrigeration system exceeds the recommended level?

A) It forms a protective layer on the system components

B) It can cause corrosion, icing, and reduced system life

C) It increases the system's efficiency

D) It helps in maintaining the lubricant's viscosity

Question 265

How can the presence of moisture in a refrigeration system be recognized?

A) The system will operate at a lower pressure than normal

B) The system will stop due to high suction pressure

C) The system will experience intermittent cooling

D) The system will have a higher than normal refrigerant charge

Question 266

What can happen if the moisture in a refrigeration system reaches a subzero temperature?

A) It can freeze and block the refrigerant flow

B) It will evaporate and leave the system

C) It will form a protective layer on the system components

D) It will react with the refrigerant to increase its efficiency

Question 267

What is the primary impact of non-condensable gases in a refrigeration system?

A) They improve the cooling capacity

B) They reduce the discharge pressure

C) They increase the system's efficiency

D) They reduce the cooling capacity and system efficiency

Question 268

In what way do non-condensable gases infiltrate sealed refrigeration systems?

A) They are introduced during equipment manufacture or servicing and remain due to incomplete evacuation

B) They are formed from chemical reactions between refrigerants and lubricants during operation

C) They are introduced through high side leakage points

D) They are desorbed from various system materials at low temperatures

Question 269

What type of flexible refrigerant pipe allows for vibration isolation?

A) Hard-drawn copper tubing

B) Threaded steel pipe

C) Corrugated stainless steel tubing

D) Soft annealed copper tubing

Question 270

Which type of central air conditioning system best supports internal humidification?

A) Package unit

B) Through-the-wall unit

C) Ductless mini-split

D) Variable refrigerant flow

PIPING AND DUCT SIZING QUESTIONS

Question 271

Which of the following is the most important factor in determining duct size?

A) Number of supply registers

B) Total cooling capacity

C) Length of duct run

D) Airflow requirements

Question 272

What formula is used to calculate duct velocity?

A) Cubic Feet per Minute / Cross-sectional area

B) Cross-sectional area x Velocity

C) Velocity x Length

D) CFM x Length

Question 273

What maximum velocity is generally recommended for supply ducts?

A) 500 fpm

B) 1000 fpm

C) 1500 fpm

D) 2000 fpm

Question 274

What refrigerant pipe sizing chart accounts for pressure drops through components?

A) Manufacturer selection chart

B) Pressure drop chart

C) Velocity chart

D) Friction loss chart

Question 275

What is the most common method used to size suction lines?

A) Diameter ratio

B) Length method

C) Capacity method

D) Velocity method

Question 276

What affects the allowed velocity in ductwork?

A) Duct material

B) Duct insulation

C) Duct shape

D) All of the above

Question 277

What duct shape has the greatest pressure loss for a given size?

A) Round

B) Rectangular

C) Oval

D) Square

Question 278

Why would an A/C system use a drier in the liquid line?

A) Prevent pipe corrosion

B) Increase oil return

C) Absorb moisture

D) Strengthen piping

Question 279

What component do pipe sizing methods not account for pressure drops through?

A) Valves

B) Fittings

C) Compressors

D) Evaporators

Question 280

What type of fitting causes the greatest pressure loss in pipes?

A) Elbow

B) Tee

C) Coupling

D) Straight pipe

Question 281

What pipe material has the lowest friction coefficient?

A) Plastic

B) Copper

C) Aluminum

D) Steel

Question 282

Why would a system use sweat fittings instead of compression fittings?

A) Easier installation

B) Lower pressure rating

C) Tighter joints

D) Improved appearance

Question 283

What material are flared fittings typically made of?

A) Plastic

B) Brass

C) Steel

D) Copper

Question 284

What type of tubing requires the use of brazing alloy and torch for joining?

A) PEX

B) Flexible refrigerant pipe

C) Copper tubing

D) PVC

Question 285

Which refrigerant pipe fitting provides the least impedance to flow?

A) Elbow

B) Tee

C) Coupling

D) Straight connecting tube

Question 286

What is used to size air conditioning condensate drain lines?

A) Inside pipe diameter

B) Outside pipe diameter

C) Pressure rating

D) Material type

AC CONTROL SYSTEMS QUESTIONS

Question 287

Which type of HVAC control system uses air pressure and pneumatic tubing for control signals?

A) Digital

B) Pneumatic

C) BACnet

D) Modbus

Question 288

What component is used in pneumatic control systems to convert an electrical signal to a pneumatic pressure signal?

A) Thermostat

B) Actuator

C) Transmitter

D) Sensor

Question 289

Which protocol is commonly used for communication between components in IP-based building controls?

A) BACnet

B) LonWorks

C) Modbus

D) ZigBee

Question 290

What component directly responds to control signals by opening and closing?

A) Sensor

B) Zone damper

C) Controller

D) Actuator

Question 291

What type of sensor measures current temperature to provide feedback to the controller?

A) RTD

B) Thermocouple

C) Thermistor

D) Pressure transducer

Question 292

What device allows remote monitoring and configuration of building controls via the internet?

A) Gateways

B) Router

C) Controller

D) Actuator

Question 293

Which HVAC system can be accurately controlled with the smallest number of sensors?

A) VAV

B) Dual duct

C) Constant volume

D) Heat pump

Question 294

Building automation systems integrate controls for what three key areas?

A) HVAC, stairs, elevators

B) HVAC, lighting, power

C) Plumbing, fire, BMS

D) Security, telecoms, HVAC

HVAC TECHNOLOGIES QUESTIONS

Question 295

What technology uses multiple indoor units connected to a single outdoor unit with refrigerant and drainage pipes?

A) VRF

B) GSHP

C) Evaporative cooling

D) Dedicated outdoor air units

Question 296

Which technology directly cools air through the evaporation of water?

A) Desiccant dehumidification

B) Evaporative cooling

C) Geothermal heating and cooling

D) Radiant heating

Question 297

Which zero ozone depletion refrigerant is gaining popularity in new HVAC systems?

A) R-134a

B) R-410A

C) R-32

D) CO2

Question 298

Which sustainable HVAC technology recovers and reuses waste heat from electronics, lighting or machinery?

A) Thermosyphon heating

B) Heat recovery chillers

C) Solar updraft towers

D) Thermoelectric generation

Question 299

What emerging smart sensor technology is able to self-power wireless sensors and transmit data?

A) Internet of Things

B) Edge computing

C) Energy harvesting

D) Distributed control

Question 300

Which advanced HVAC option optimizes for individual comfort using personal IoT devices and predictive analytics?

A) Occupant-centered controls

B) Multi-split VRF

C) Hybrid geothermal

D) Low-exergy systems

Question 301

What is the process of utilizing waste heat to pre-heat air prior to conditioning?

A) Run-around heat recovery

B) Heat pipes

C) Thermosyphons

D) Evaporative pre-cooling

Question 302

What technology can provide simultaneous heating/cooling via a single water connection instead of refrigerants?

A) VRF systems

B) Hydronic radiant systems

C) Thermoelectric A/C

D) Geothermal heat pumps

ANSWERS

Question	Answer
AIR CONDITIONERS GENERAL QUESTIONS	
1. Which of the following best defines "HVACR"?	B) Heating, ventilation, air-conditioning, and refrigeration
2. What are the three main classifications of air conditioners according to function?	B) Cooling, heat pump, geothermal
3. What sensor controls the operation of the central air conditioning system?	A) Thermostat
4. Which component removes heat from the refrigerant?	A) Condenser
5. What is the function of the indoor coil in the air handler unit?	B) It evaporates refrigerant to absorb heat
6. What controls airflow through the evaporator coil and into the ductwork?	C) Blower fan
7. What type of air conditioner utilizes both an electric heater and a heat pump for heating?	C) Cooling/heating
8. What units are commonly used to measure cooling capacity?	D) BTU/hr and Kw
9. What factor most influences heating equipment size for a space?	B) Floor plan
10. Through-the-wall units have what positioned on both the indoor and outdoor sides?	C) Fans
11. What type of latent heat occurs when a refrigerant changes from a gas to a liquid?	A) Condensation latent heat
12. What is the standard unit of measurement in the US for heat flow?	B) BTU
13. What is one ton of refrigeration equivalent to in terms of cooling capacity?	A) 12,000 BTU/hr
14. What is relative humidity a measure of?	D) Ratio of actual vapor pressure to saturation pressure
15. How many BTUs per hour are needed to heat a typical 200 sq ft bedroom?	A) 10,000-15,000
16. What percentage of total heat loss occurs through an average home's walls?	C) 30-35%
17. What determines the evaporating temperature in the evaporator coil?	A) Return air temperature
18. What should be checked prior to any AC service call?	A) Filters
19. What tool is used to recover refrigerant from an AC system?	B) Vacuum pump
20. Why is airflow volume important when servicing an AC unit?	D) System balance
21. What should be checked when diagnosing insufficient cooling?	C) Superheat and subcooling
22. What device identifies refrigerant type in AC systems?	B) Manifold gauge set

23. Which of the following would be considered personal protective equipment?	C) Safety glasses
24. What type of equipment is required for use with ammonia refrigerant?	B) Respiratory protection equipment
25. What equipment is necessary to remove refrigerant from a system in a controlled manner?	B) Recovery unit
26. What are the three main components of a central air conditioning system?	B) Compressor, condenser, evaporator
27. What type of protective equipment is needed when handling phosphorus or silver brazing alloys?	D) Face shield
28. Which tool is uniquely suited for bending soft copper refrigerant lines?	C) Pipe bender
29. What type of equipment monitors for the presence of hydrocarbon refrigerants?	A) Gas detector
30. What attachment on a recovery machine is used to puncture access fittings to begin recovery?	A) Recovery piercing pliers
31. What piece of auxiliary equipment is necessary to braze copper refrigerant lines?	C) Torch
32. What type of fan is commonly used for supply air in residential ducted systems?	What type of fan is commonly used for supply air in residential ducted systems?
33. What aspect of fan performance defines how much air it can move at a given power input?	C) Efficiency
34. What pump circulates hot or cold water between an air handler and connected terminals?	B) Circulator pump
35. What pump moves air through the indoor and outdoor coils of a split system AC?	A) Blower fan
36. What circulating pump type is continuous, quiet and self-priming for HVAC use?	D) In-line pump
37. What is the process of verifying and documenting that all building systems and components are installed correctly and function according to design intent?	C) Commissioning
38. What diagnostic tools capture infrared emissions to detect thermal irregularities in HVAC equipment?	D) Thermography
39. What device measures amperage to identify undersized circuit breakers or overloading?	B) Ammeter
40. What device measures subcooling and superheat when troubleshooting refrigerant issues?	C) Refrigerant gauges
41. What device measures static and dynamic air pressures during ductwork testing?	C) Manometer
42. What device passes a puff of non-toxic smoke to detect abnormal air leakage locations?	B) Duct blaster

LIFE CYCLE COSTS QUESTIONS	
43. Which of the following most significantly impacts the total cost of ownership over the unit's lifespan?	C) Annual energy use
44. Replacing an evaporator coil usually occurs every _____ years on average.	A) 5-7
45. What maintenance task helps maximize equipment efficiency and lifespan?	A) Drain line cleaning
46. What system upgrade usually achieves payback in 2-5 years through energy savings?	B) Insulated ductwork
47. Which type of portable room air conditioner includes an optional humidification function?	B) Window unit
48. What system component will typically require replacement last over the equipment's life?	D) Heat exchanger
49. Why is proper equipment sizing important for optimal life-cycle performance?	D) All of the above
50. Tune-ups that include what can extend AC system life by 5-7 years?	B) Refrigerant leak checks
51. Which type of air conditioner typically includes provisions for optional humidification?	D) Central air conditioning
52. Improving what aspect of a home significantly improves HVAC life-cycle costs?	A) Insulation levels
53. What maintenance tasks typically need performed quarterly?	D) Filter replacement and coil cleaning
54. What has the greatest influence on reducing runtime costs each month?	D) Thermostat programming
55. On average, what does replacing an old A/C unit save annually through lower utility bills?	C) $500-800
HVACR INDUSTRY QUESTIONS	
56. Which of the following best defines the role of trade associations in the HVACR industry?	C) Lobby for legislation on behalf of member companies
57. Which of the following is NOT a difference between air conditioning and heating?	D) Primary system components
58. What does "PAHRA" stand for?	B) Partnership for Air-Conditioning and Heating Regulation Accreditation
59. Which of the following best describes the role of PAHRA in the HVACR industry?	D) Awards accreditation to education programs meeting industry standards
60. Ventilation is often inadequate because:	A) Buildings have become too airtight
61. What is the primary purpose of the HVAC assessments?	B) To evaluate mastery of skills for specific craft roles
62. What is considered the high side of a refrigeration system?	A) The condenser and the liquid line
AIR CONDITIONING SYSTEM DESIGN QUESTIONS	
63. Which of the following is the most common cooling option used when conditioned air is required for an air handling unit?	D) Air coils using site water below 65°F
64. What is the main difference between air conditioning and refrigeration?	A) Air conditioning cools and dehumidifies the air, while refrigeration only cools and freezes

65. What is a key difference between the circulation systems of air conditioning and refrigeration?	D) Air conditioning requires a fan, while refrigeration does not require a fan
66. Which air conditioning system is suitable for providing individual temperature control in different zones or rooms, and consists of an outdoor compressor/condenser and indoor air-handling units?	C) Ductless Mini-Split
67. What should be considered when selecting the location of an outdoor unit?	C) Installing in an area protected from wind
68. What type of refrigerant is commonly used in small air conditioning systems?	C) R-22
69. What is the refrigerant known for its lower Global Warming Potential (GWP) and used as a lower GWP solution for air conditioning?	B) R-32
70. Which of the following types of HVAC equipment is commonly used when air is cooled with 100% unconditioned outdoor air?	B) Direct evaporative cooling units
71. What is the preferred air distribution method?	D) Supply air to lower levels and return from upper levels
72. What is the purpose of a VAV (Variable Air Volume) box in HVAC systems?	B) To regulate the airflow
73. Which of the following locations is recommended by the document for intake louvers?	B) Opposite heat sources
74. Complete HVAC system redundancy generally involves:	A) Two equally sized systems capable of the full load
75. What scale is used to rate the moisture removal capacity of air conditioners and dehumidifiers?	B) Pints per day
76. What component found in some PTAC units improves dehumidification performance?	C) Dehumidifying coil
EPA SECTION 608 QUESTIONS	
77. Which of the following best describes the type of refrigerant that has been shown to be the most destructive to stratospheric ozone?	D) Refrigerants containing bromine.
78. EPA regulations require technicians to demonstrate the ability to perform which refrigerant handling procedure?	A) Recovery
79. What is the term used to describe the purity standard refrigerant must meet to be considered reclaimed?	A) ARI-700 standard
80. According to the Montreal Protocol, which of the following substances is NOT controlled?	C) Carbon dioxide
81. What is the length of time refrigerant recovered from a system less than 1 year old can be called reclaimed?	C) It can never be called reclaimed
82. Which part of a vapor compression system changes the low pressure vapor to a high pressure vapor?	D) Compressor

83. Which of the following best describes an azeotropic refrigerant mixture?	C) A mixture that acts as a single component refrigerant
84. Which of the following is true about blended refrigerants leaking from a system?	B) They leak slower than other refrigerants
85. Which of the following devices is used to reduce the pressure of refrigerant vapor?	B) Expansion device
86. What does an HFC refrigerant contain?	A) Hydrogen, fluorine, carbon
87. According to the EPA, when must an oil sample be taken from a system?	D) After a major leak or component failure
88. What type of refrigerant requires the most amount of pressure to change from a liquid to a vapor?	C) CFC
89. Which part of a vapor compression system converts high pressure vapor back to high pressure liquid?	B) Condenser
90. Which of the following best describes the motive behind the Montreal Protocol?	C) To control the production of ozone depleting substances
91. Which of the following parts would not be considered required by EPA regulations for all air conditioning and refrigeration systems using CFCs, HCFCs or HFCs?	A) Thermostatic expansion valve
92. What is the term used to describe the process of cleaning a refrigerant to reduce moisture and acidity?	C) Recycling
93. What type of equipment relies on the compressor in the existing system to perform recovery?	B) System-dependent recovery units
94. According to ASHRAE safety classification, which designation indicates the most unsafe refrigerant?	D) B-3
95. When would it be acceptable to vent small amounts of refrigerant according to EPA regulations?	C) In the normal operation of an appliance
96. Which of the following best describes the requirement for hydrostatic testing of reusable cylinders?	B) Every 5 years
97. Which part of a vapor compression system absorbs heat from the refrigerated space?	B) Evaporator
98. What is the term used to describe the process that returns refrigerant to new product specifications through chemical analysis and purity testing?	B) Reclamation
99. What is considered the most effective method for detecting small refrigerant leaks according to the EPA?	C) Electronic or ultrasonic detection
100. How many ozone molecules can each chlorine atom in the stratosphere destroy?	D) 100,000
101. Which of the following best characterizes a self-contained recovery device?	B) Can capture refrigerant in liquid or vapor form without external equipment

102. What is the term used to describe the quantitative rating of a refrigerant's ability to deplete stratospheric ozone?	B) Ozone depletion potential
103. What should Technicians never do when using dry nitrogen to pressurize a system?	A) Charge as a liquid
104. What device is used to safely reduce the pressure in a refrigerant cylinder before disposal?	C) Pressure regulator
105. Which of the following best characterizes a non-azeotropic refrigerant mixture?	D) Composition changes with temperature
106. What should technicians do before opening a refrigeration system or disposing of its components?	A) Recover any remaining refrigerant
107. Which of the following is used to improve the sensitivity of leak detectors?	A) Bromomethane tracer gas
108. When should an oil sample be taken from a system according to EPA guidelines?	B) After a catastrophic failure
109. What is considered the proper method of removing all refrigerant from a system or component?	C) Evacuation to a hard vacuum
110. What type of equipment can capture refrigerant in either liquid or vapor form without relying on system components?	C) System-independent recovery machines
111. Non-condensable gases such as air prevent which part of the vapor compression process from working properly?	B) Condensation
112. According to the Montreal Protocol, which is considered less damaging to stratospheric ozone than CFCs?	C) HCFCs
113. What type of halogenated substance is R-141b?	A) HCFC
114. When using compressed gas for leak detection or system pressure, technicians should use:	D) Nitrogen
115. Which component commonly causes moisture to migrate into the compressor crankcase?	D) Evaporator
116. What term describes the process of achieving a vacuum that prohibits the flow of air and non-condensable gases into the system?	C) Evacuation
117. When should recovery and recycling equipment be certified according to the EPA?	D) Every 5 years
TEST PROCEDURES	
118. According to the current test procedures, which of the following split system types can be tested?	B) Multi-split, multi-head mini-split, and multi-circuit systems
119. Testing variable capacity AC units at part load conditions according to the US test procedure has proven:	C) Problematic and inaccurate

120. What does 10 CFR 430 Subpart B primarily address?	A) Energy consumption of household appliances
121. What is the document that provides detailed inspection checklists and test worksheets for the functional inspection and testing of HVAC systems?	B) HVAC Functional Inspection and Testing Guide
122. Which of the following refrigerants has the highest critical pressure?	B) Ammonia
123. Where does the lowest temperature occur in a vapour compression cycle?	C) Evaporator
124. What is the leading efficiency metric used for minimum standards and energy guide labels for room air conditioners?	C) Seasonal Energy Efficiency Ratio (SEER)
125. What governs heat transfer through convection?	A) Density differences
126. What is the purpose of the cycling test in air conditioner testing?	B) To assess the system's performance during part-load operation and temperature changes
HVAC SYSTEMS BACKGROUND	
127. What is the unit of heat?	C) BTU
128. Which of the following is NOT a mechanism of heat transfer?	C) Evaporation
129. Which of the following best defines the humidity ratio?	A) Weight of water vapor per unit weight of dry air
130. What temperature scale has its freezing point defined at 0°C and boiling point at 100°C?	D) Celsius
131. What is the room sensible heat factor used for in air conditioning systems?	B) Calculating the heat gain from occupants and lights
132. What is the primary factor that influences the design of an AC system in a residential setting?	D) Cooling loads
133. Which of the following is essential for ensuring good indoor air quality and efficient air distribution in an AC system design?	B) Ventilation and ducts
134. What is the purpose of equipment sizing in the design of an AC system?	C) To determine the type and size of the system
135. What type of heat is involved when a refrigerant changes from a gas to a liquid?	A) Latent heat
136. Why is proper ductwork design important in the AC system design for a residential setting?	C) To achieve even comfort throughout the home
137. Which type of AC system has two units for cooling and heating, and is commonly found in residential settings?	A) Traditional Split System
138. Which type of air conditioning system is often used in residential settings where space for indoor components is limited?	D) Packaged System
139. Which of the following best defines sensible heat?	A) Heat that increases temperature but not humidity
140. Sensible heat is determined by which property of air?	A) Temperature

141. What is the temperature range of the standard psychrometric chart for air conditioning?	D) 32 to 120°F
142. Which of the following is NOT one of the purposes of an HVAC system?	C) Increase relative humidity
143. Which psychrometric process increases both temperature and moisture content?	D) Humidification
144. What is considered the boundary that separates the indoor and outdoor environment?	A) Building air barrier
145. What type of ventilation strategy utilizes both supply and exhaust fans?	B) Balanced
146. Which of the following best summarizes the primary function of an HVAC system?	B) To maintain occupant comfort in a conditioned space.
147. Which of the following is NOT a consideration in properly designing an air conditioning system?	C) Cost of annual maintenance
148. What year did the American Society of Heating and Ventilating Engineers (ASH&VE) form?	A) 1894
149. What was one of the earliest key developments in improving combustion heating systems according to the passage?	A) Addition of fans to furnace systems
150. Which of the following best defines the Energy Star program mentioned in the passage?	D) A standard that rates building energy performance compared to national averages
151. Which of the following factors would NOT affect the performance of an HVAC system?	D) Amount of outdoor shade trees
152. Which type of ventilation system removes air from specific rooms or areas using a local exhaust fan?	C) Spot ventilation
153. Which type of HVAC system provides conditioned air to each room using supply and return registers?	A) Forced air system
154. Which of the following is NOT considered an important design concept for energy efficient design?	B) Maintaining complexity
155. Which of the following is considered a key element of sustainable design?	D) Efficient use of energy resources
156. Which of the following best defines the LEED program?	B) A voluntary standard for sustainable building design and construction
157. According to the second law of thermodynamics, which of the following cannot occur naturally without effort expended somewhere?	B) The mixing of two gases
158. Which process/scenario BEST represents an irreversible process?	A) The natural mixing of two gases in contact
159. Which of the following processes involves NO transfer of heat?	C) Adiabatic
160. Below which pressure does water NOT exist in three phases (solid, liquid, vapor) at the same temperature?	C) Critical pressure

161. What is meant by the term "intensive property" as used in thermodynamics?	B) A property whose value is independent of the size or extent of the system
162. Which of the following scales uses degrees K as its absolute temperature units?	A) Kelvin
163. What type of HVAC system design method determines room-by-room heating and cooling loads?	B) Manual J

AIR CONDITIONING AND REFRIGERATION CALCULATION QUESTIONS

164. What is the base unit used for measuring heat in the HVAC industry?	D) BTUs
165. What is the specific heat of air in Btu/lb°F?	A) 0.24
166. What constant pressure is used to define 1 Ton of Refrigeration?	B) 14.7 psi
167. What constant is used to determine the latent heat load in Btu/h using the formula:	C) 0.68
168. What is the typical CFM produced per ton of air conditioning?	D) 400 CFM
169. What value is used for air density in most HVAC calculations in lb/ft3?	B) 0.075
170. What variable is defined as the ratio of vapor pressure to the saturation vapor pressure?	C) Relative humidity
171. What is considered the minimum CFM of airflow per 100 square feet of house floor area for proper HVAC performance?	A) 25-50 CFM
172. Which of the following is NOT considered a good location for an indoor air conditioning unit?	C) In a kitchen near cooking appliances
173. Which of the following is NOT an appropriate outdoor air design temperature to use for HVAC cooling load calculations?	C) Extreme design conditions
174. What calculation determines BTUs contained in 1 pound of a substance with a given specific heat?	A) BTU = Mass x Specific Heat x Temperature Change
175. Heat flows naturally from objects at what temperature to objects at what lower temperature?	C) Higher to lower

AIR CONDITIONING SYSTEM COMPONENTS

176. What device senses and controls room temperature?	A) Thermostat
177. What type of compressor is commonly used in air conditioners?	C) Reciprocating compressor
178. What component is located entirely on the interior side of the wall?	D) Evaporator coil
179. What device regulates the flow of refrigerant into the evaporator?	A) Capillary tube
180. What is the purpose of a strainer in an AC system?	C) To remove foreign particles from the refrigerant
181. What allows the compressor to start under high load conditions?	C) Hard start kit

#	Question	Answer
182.	What device protects the compressor from overload?	C) Overload protector
183.	What device senses room temperature and controls the compressor?	A) Thermistor
184.	What determines the evaporating temperature of the refrigerant in the evaporator?	B) Suction pressure
185.	How are indoor units typically installed?	C) Suspended from the ceiling
186.	What tool is used to accurately measure refrigerant pressures?	D) Manometer
187.	When installing an indoor unit, what is important to consider for adequate air circulation?	B) Minimum specified clearance
188.	What type of thermostat directly controls single speed compressor units?	D) Mechanical
189.	What device is used to control the flow of liquid refrigerant into the evaporator?	D) Expansion Valve
190.	What process causes the high pressure refrigerant liquid to change to low pressure in the capillary tube?	D) Expansion
191.	What type of heat is released in the condenser?	A) Latent heat
192.	What device is used to separate any liquid refrigerant from the suction line vapor before entering the compressor?	A) Accumulator
193.	What property of R-22 allows it to absorb a large amount of heat with little rise in temperature in the evaporator?	C) High heat of vaporization
194.	What component receives the high pressure, high temperature vapor from the condenser?	C) Compressor
195.	What causes an increase in pressure when the refrigerant is compressed in the compressor?	B) Volume decrease

TYPES OF AIR CONDITIONING UNITS

#	Question	Answer
196.	What allows installation and removal of a window unit from the outside of a building?	A) Sliding frame assembly
197.	What device controls moisture removal in the indoor coil of a window unit?	B) Evaporator coil
198.	What device controls the degree of air circulation throughout a room?	D) Louver blades
199.	Where is the thermostat sensor typically located on a window unit?	C) Near the evaporator coil
200.	What is the recommended first step before purchasing a window air conditioning unit for your home?	A) Measure the size and shape of your windows
201.	What is the common cause of leaking water in a window air conditioning unit?	D) Condensation on the evaporator coil

202. What is the recommended action to prevent air leaks when installing a window air conditioning unit?	B) Seal the window with accordion panels
203. Which of the following is a unique element of split air conditioners?	A) They have to be drained periodically
204. What is one of the main advantages of a multi split system air conditioner?	B) It can only cool the rooms you need to, saving money and energy
205. What is a common problem that can arise due to irregular maintenance of a split air conditioner?	C) Lack of cooling
206. What is a characteristic of the outdoor unit in a split air conditioning system?	B) It houses the compressor and condenser
207. What type of fan is commonly used in indoor split units?	C) Axial
208. What provides auxiliary heating for certain split systems?	B) Electric coil
209. What type of resistance heating element is common for auxiliary heat?	D) Calrod
210. What type of HVAC system contains all refrigerant circuit components within one factory-made enclosure?	C) Packaged terminal AC
211. What type of piping is typically used for refrigerant lines in packaged units?	B) Brazed joints
212. How is conditioned air distributed from packaged terminal ACs?	D) Ductwork
213. What allows packaged rooftop units to cool multiple zones?	A) Variable speed fan
214. What directs air into the building through a ceiling tile or wall sleeve?	D) Discharge grille
215. What devices sense return air conditions on some packaged units?	A) Thermistors
SYSTEM SERVICE AND REPAIR QUESTIONS	
216. Why should non-condensibles be removed prior to system repair?	C) Inhibit heat transfer
217. What is used to convert a system to an alternative refrigerant?	B) Retrofit kit
218. Why should lubricant be changed during retrofit procedures?	A) Incompatibility with new refrigerant
219. What information is required for environmentally responsible reclamation?	C) Refrigerant composition
220. What causes the pressure on the high side of an air conditioning system to rise rapidly leading to a condition known as "slugging"?	A) Clogged filter/drier
221. What component acts as a sort of "shock absorber" in an air conditioning system and allows the compressor to operate smoothly by temporarily storing excess refrigerant during off cycles?	B) Suction accumulator

222. What is the purpose of the sight glass installed on the liquid line just before the thermostatic expansion valve in an air conditioning system?	A) Indicates refrigerant charge level
223. What is the normal operating pressure range at ambient temperature of 90°F for an R-22 AC with a 15 SEER rating?	A) 175-225 psig
224. What causes abnormally high head (high side) pressure in an air conditioning system?	C) Non-condensable gases
225. What component detects excessively low or high refrigerant pressures and shuts down the compressor for safety?	B) Pressure control switch
226. What condition or defect would cause the evaporator coil leaving air temperature to be warmer than normal?	C) Low refrigerant charge
227. What are small ports or holes connected to suction and discharge lines of an air conditioning compressor used for?	C) Oil equalization
228. An accumulation of what substance on outdoor AC units reduces efficiency by preventing heat transfer?	D) Mineral deposits
229. During a/c system repair, what should be performed prior to evacuating moisture from the system?	D) Recovering refrigerant
230. What type of filter is typically found in an indoor air handler or furnace to catch dust and debris from returning air?	C) Pleated paper
231. What device protects the compressor from liquid refrigerant by temporarily storing it during off cycles?	A) Accumulator
232. What is the most common cause of air conditioning compressor failure?	B) Lack of maintenance
233. What device uses subcooling to regulate refrigerant flow into an evaporator coil?	A) TXV
AC FAULT DIAGNOSIS QUESTIONS	
234. What is the most likely cause if an AC unit trips the breaker whenever turned on?	A) Damaged start capacitor
235. A home AC unit is producing warm air from vents. What should be checked first?	C) Thermostat calibration
236. AC runs but the home does not cool down. What is a possible cause?	B) Refrigerant leak
237. AC unit blows warm air on one side of home. What diagnostic step should be taken?	D) Examine zone dampers
238. AC unit blows humid air and water droplets form on supply vents. What is likely faulty?	B) Drain line restriction
239. AC unit frequently cycles on and off. What can potentially remedy this?	C) Check superheat setting
240. AC unit blows warm air and makes buzzing noise. What component may be faulty?	D) Capacitor

#	Question	Answer
241.	AC unit blows warm air with ice forming on evap coils. What should be checked?	A) Airflow across coils
242.	AC unit blows 70 degrees air on warm days. What may cause this?	C) Thermostat stuck closed
243.	AC unit blows warm air when changing to cool mode. First inspect which component?	A) Filter
244.	On a hot day, the system pressure rises high but cycling cutout doesn't function. What could be faulty?	D) High pressure control
245.	The AC unit blows 66°F air on 95°F day. Subcooling is normal but suction pressure is low. What could be the problem?	A) Leaking TXV

REFRIGERANT SPECIFIC QUESTIONS

#	Question	Answer
246.	Which ISO standard addresses the designation and classification of refrigerants?	A) ISO 817
247.	What does ISO 916 cover in relation to refrigeration systems?	D) Technical performance testing
248.	What does the LFL value indicate for refrigerant flammability classification?	B) Lowest concentration required for ignition
249.	Is it possible for a refrigerant to be considered non-toxic?	B) No
250.	What standard does the refrigerant numbering classification system follow?	C) ASHRAE 34
251.	Which lubricant property aims to prevent plugging of refrigerant control components?	A) Low wax content
252.	Which property maintains good lubrication at high and low temperatures?	C) Low viscosity index
253.	What is the overall goal of containment and leak detection?	C) Minimize refrigerant releases
254.	According to the ISO 11650 standard, what does recovery involve?	A) Removing refrigerant and storing it externally
255.	How is recovered refrigerant stored according to the same standard as above?	D) Externally to the system
256.	Where does recycling typically take place?	C) At the field job site
257.	What is the primary purpose of refrigerant recovery equipment?	C) To temporarily store recovered refrigerant
258.	Which method of refrigerant recovery is recommended for liquid refrigerant transfer from an AC system?	C) Push-pull transfer
259.	What is the purpose of purging in the servicing of a refrigeration system?	A) To remove non-condensable gases
260.	When charging refrigerants, why is it important to follow the manufacturer's specifications?	C) To ensure proper system performance and efficiency
261.	Which of the following is a purpose of flaring in tubing techniques for refrigeration systems?	C) To create a seal with another fitting
262.	What is the main function of a manifold gauge in refrigeration servicing?	D) To measure the system's pressure

263. What is the main reason why moisture is difficult to eliminate from a refrigeration system?	A) It is essentially dissolved in the refrigerant
264. What can happen if the moisture concentration in a refrigeration system exceeds the recommended level?	B) It can cause corrosion, icing, and reduced system life
265. How can the presence of moisture in a refrigeration system be recognized?	C) The system will experience intermittent cooling
266. What can happen if the moisture in a refrigeration system reaches a subzero temperature?	A) It can freeze and block the refrigerant flow
267. What is the primary impact of non-condensable gases in a refrigeration system?	D) They reduce the cooling capacity and system efficiency
268. In what way do non-condensable gases infiltrate sealed refrigeration systems?	A) They are introduced during equipment manufacture or servicing and remain due to incomplete evacuation
269. What type of flexible refrigerant pipe allows for vibration isolation?	C) Corrugated stainless steel tubing
270. Which type of central air conditioning system best supports internal humidification?	D) Variable refrigerant flow
PIPING AND DUCT SIZING QUESTIONS	
271. Which of the following is the most important factor in determining duct size?	D) Airflow requirements
272. What formula is used to calculate duct velocity?	A) Cubic Feet per Minute / Cross-sectional area
273. What maximum velocity is generally recommended for supply ducts?	B) 1000 fpm
274. What refrigerant pipe sizing chart accounts for pressure drops through components?	D) Friction loss chart
275. What is the most common method used to size suction lines?	A) Diameter ratio
276. What affects the allowed velocity in ductwork?	D) All of the above
277. What duct shape has the greatest pressure loss for a given size?	B) Rectangular
278. Why would an A/C system use a drier in the liquid line?	C) Absorb moisture
279. What component do pipe sizing methods not account for pressure drops through?	C) Compressors
280. What type of fitting causes the greatest pressure loss in pipes?	B) Tee
281. What pipe material has the lowest friction coefficient?	A) Plastic
282. Why would a system use sweat fittings instead of compression fittings?	C) Tighter joints
283. What material are flared fittings typically made of?	B) Brass
284. What type of tubing requires the use of brazing alloy and torch for joining?	C) Copper tubing
285. Which refrigerant pipe fitting provides the	D) Straight connecting tube

least impedance to flow?	
286. What is used to size air conditioning condensate drain lines?	A) Inside pipe diameter
AC CONTROL SYSTEMS	
287. Which type of HVAC control system uses air pressure and pneumatic tubing for control signals?	B) Pneumatic
288. What component is used in pneumatic control systems to convert an electrical signal to a pneumatic pressure signal?	C) Transmitter
289. Which protocol is commonly used for communication between components in IP-based building controls?	A) BACnet
290. What component directly responds to control signals by opening and closing?	D) Actuator
291. What type of sensor measures current temperature to provide feedback to the controller?	C) Thermistor
292. What device allows remote monitoring and configuration of building controls via the internet?	A) Gateways
293. Which HVAC system can be accurately controlled with the smallest number of sensors?	A) VAV
294. Building automation systems integrate controls for what three key areas?	B) HVAC, lighting, power
HVAC TECHNOLOGIES	
295. What technology uses multiple indoor units connected to a single outdoor unit with refrigerant and drainage pipes?	A) VRF
296. Which technology directly cools air through the evaporation of water?	B) Evaporative cooling
297. Which zero ozone depletion refrigerant is gaining popularity in new HVAC systems?	C) R-32
298. Which sustainable HVAC technology recovers and reuses waste heat from electronics, lighting or machinery?	B) Heat recovery chillers
299. What emerging smart sensor technology is able to self-power wireless sensors and transmit data?	B) Edge computing
300. Which advanced HVAC option optimizes for individual comfort using personal IoT devices and predictive analytics?	A) Occupant-centered controls
301. What is the process of utilizing waste heat to pre-heat air prior to conditioning?	A) Run-around heat recovery
302. What technology can provide simultaneous heating/cooling via a single water connection instead of refrigerants?	B) Hydronic radiant systems

Printed in Dunstable, United Kingdom